Congregational Evangelism

A Pastor's View

■

The Denman Lectures 1992

MAXIE D. DUNNAM

DISCIPLESHIP RESOURCES

MATERIALS FOR GROWTH IN CHRISTIAN FAITH AND LIFE

P.O. Box 189 • Nashville, TN 37023 • 615-340-7284

Cover and text design by Ruth Farwell.

ISBN 0-88177-116-3

Library of Congress Catalog Card Number: 92-71108

DR116B

DEDICATION

Had not certain preachers been part of my life,
I would not have been a person invited
to deliver the Denman Lectures.
I dedicate this book to them.

Ira Gallaway
Joe Hale
Eddie Fox
Danny Morris
Rueben Job
Wilson Weldon
Edward Tullis

CONTENTS

PREFACE

Harry Denman is among the most outstanding Christians I have known. To describe someone as "an outstanding Christian" may not be appropriate. I mean that Harry was totally committed to Christ. In some quarters, one might say he was "sold out to Jesus."

Harry's specific vocation as a Christian was "evangelist." He never ignored an opportunity to witness for Jesus Christ. It is appropriate that The Foundation for Evangelism has established a lectureship in his memory. To have been invited to deliver those lectures is a signal honor for me, yet a humbling experience. To have those lectures published adds to my feeling of gratitude.

This book is the content of those lectures. Little has been added or deleted, and very little has been done to alter the text from a spoken to a written style.

Since my theme is the congregation as evangelist, integrity demanded that my local church be the proving ground and the setting out of which the illustrative stories came. Some of them may have been used in other sermons, lectures, or printed material. I deliberately did not change that because I wanted to make my case as clearly and powerfully as possible.

I am convinced that unless and until pastors of local congregations see themselves as responsible, and grasp the exciting challenge and opportunity of evangelism, Methodism (our denominational branch of the church) will not be renewed and we will continue to decline in membership, mission, and ministry.

I am aware that every congregation is unique and the possibilities for mission and ministry vary. I do not believe, however, that there is any church anywhere void of opportunities to evangelize in some way. The specific way we do it at Christ Church in Memphis, Tennessee may not be appropriate any place else. But the model of the congregation as the "people of God" and/or "the Body of Christ," if actualized, will define the audience for our witness where we are, and shape our ministry and mission.

I'm deeply grateful to Bishop Earl Hunt and the Foundation for trusting me with this awesome task. I'm grateful to Dr. Craig Gallaway, Editorial Director of Discipleship Resources, not only for pushing the notion that these lectures should be published, but for his contribution to their shaping, and his editorial work in preparing them for publication. In the process, he has become a valued friend.

Had I not been privileged to serve as pastor of Christ United Methodist Church in Memphis for these past ten years, I would not have the experiential stuff that gives whatever authenticity and liveliness these lectures have. So, I'm grateful for a congregation in which there are many disciples reaching to make disciples.

If anything here inspires and equips anyone for doing evangelism, I will be pleased. Harry Denman will be also.

M. D. D.
Memphis, Tennessee
Spring 1992

FOREWORD

Maxie D. Dunnam, the 1992 Denman Lecturer, is the senior pastor of Christ United Methodist Church in Memphis, Tennessee, the largest United Methodist congregation in the Volunteer State. He was formerly World Editor of The Upper Room, is a prolific author, and has pioneered with remarkable success in the field of audiovisual communication of United Methodism. Dr. Dunnam has also been a vigorous leader in the work of The World Methodist Council, a member of its Executive Committee, and chair of the Program Committee which planned the World Methodist Conference held in Nairobi in 1986.

Dr. Dunnam's has been an unusually productive career in many arenas of the Christian ministry, particularly in preaching, writing, and programming. He has brought to his task a mind grounded in the fundamentals of classical Christian theology, the capacity to achieve fresh and imaginative perspectives upon contemporary life and faith, and an indefatigable verve which seems to dance with energy and purpose.

This lectureship honors the memory of one of the most influential and picturesque evangelists in the history of our church. Harry Denman, a layman, came in mature life from the business world into full-time Christian service. He began his church career as business manager for First Church in Birmingham, Alabama; and, in 1938, became associated with the staff of the Department of Evangelism in the Board of Missions of the Methodist Episcopal Church, South. A year later, with the unification of the three branches of American Methodism, he was named secretary of the Commission on Evangelism. In 1944 he became the first General Secretary of the General Board of Evangelism of The Methodist Church, a position he held until his retirement in 1965. In this office, he developed a fledgling staff into one of the largest, most highly motivated, and most effective leadership groups in the entire denomination.

His own fame as a lay evangelist spread with each succeeding year, partly as a result of the clear and pratical way in which he preached the gospel and shared Jesus Christ; but also because of his transparent personal dedication and, perhaps, certain endearing eccentricities. He believed that he should own no more clothing than was required to keep him presentable, warm, and clean; and he traveled all over the world with a single suit of clothes, a top coat in colder weather, two shirts, and a change of underwear and socks. He owned no property but made his home, when he was not on journeys, a simple apartment in Nashville.

He was political strategist par excellence, and his wise and effective leadership in many General Conferences left an enduring impression upon our church. It was he who, in 1949, caused The Foundation for Evangelism to be created as an agency related to the General Board of Evangelism (now Discipleship) and commissioned to help enable that Board to do the things for which its own budget could make no adequate provision. A legend in his own time, Harry Denman was one of the most greatly beloved leaders the Methodist movement has ever had. The Denman Lectures, a project of The Foundation for Evangelism, were established in order to pay tribute to his life and, later, his memory.

Across the years, the Denman Lectures, always featured at the biennial Congress on Evangelism, have been given by a galaxy of renowned leaders in our denomination, including the late Dr. Albert C. Outler, Bishop Wayne K. Clymer, Sir Alan Walker, Bishop Roy Nichols, Dr. Ellsworth Kalas, Professor George E. Morris, Dr. Joe Hale, and Bishop Emerson Colaw. Maxie Dunnam, appropriately, takes his place in what has become one of evangelism's "endless lines of splendor."

Dr. Dunnam's three lectures for 1992 were well researched, clearly written, and forcefully delivered. His wide experience as a speaker and a writer has enabled him to perfect an extremely effective dialogical style which could serve as an excellent model of contemporary Christian communication at its best. He employs an easy but dignified vernacular, and both his sermons and his manuscripts sparkle with humor and a robust form of humanness. He is, withal, a superb communicator.

The focus of all three lectures, as the author makes abundantly clear, is the local church—and it is this focus which gives the lectures their remarkable relevance. Dr. Dunnam begins with the proposition that ideas have consequences. The first and foremost proposition that he presses home in this regard is that Jesus Christ is the unique Savior of the world. Dunnam is concerned that modern religious syncretism has convinced some to diminish the stature of Jesus. His strong insistence upon the eternal uniqueness of the Savior is always unqualified and clear. He also indicts quite severely the fresh prominence which has come to the old idea of universal salvation, citing a current book on this subject by a distinguished United methodist scholar and leader.

But Dunnam's concern in this regard is not simply dogmatic—i.e., the preservation of a particular doctrinal formula. Rather, his concern is with evangelism, with the ministry and true service of the church. Thus, Dunnam argues, "What you think of Jesus Christ will determine what you do about evangelism." What Dr. Dunnam is finally after is an approach to evangelism centered in Christ, empowered by the Holy Spirit, and reaching out through the life and witness of the congregation to embrace and include the whole of creation and human society. Quoting Georgia Harkness, he asserts that "we must rescue evangelism from the red-light district of the ecclesiastical community."

Thus, in Lectures Two and Three, Dunnam focuses on the symbiosis of evangelism and discipleship. He asserts that we cannot really have one without the other. And in Lecture Three, he brings all of this to a crowning point in the recognition that evangelism in the true sense ultimately entails the whole life and witness of the congregation—in a word, the whole gospel, for the whole person, and the whole world. All of this explains why the published form of these lectures now appears under the title, *Congregational Evangelism.*

But now we must be clear about the special angle of these lectures. Many authors (pastors and theologians) have undertaken to make the case for holistic evangelism. Dunnam is fully aware of the lineage within which he stands. He insists that the evangelistic enterprise includes both personal faith *and* mission or social action, declaring that anything else constitutes a "schizoid" understanding of the gospel. He declares his own deep commitment to a holistic gospel. What gives Dunnam's lectures special brilliance, however, is his deep conviction, born from years of pastoral experience, that the essential basis of holistic evangelism is not a theory or a special principle, but the congregation itself.

For this reason, Dunnam has chosen to illustrate many of his points with stories from actual pastoral experience. (Note the subtitle of this volume: *A Pastor's View.*) Thus, to illustrate the symbiosis of evangelism and discipleship, Dunnam describes the particular design developed for the church he serves, including four separate tracks: spiritual discipline and growth, Bible-theology, applied discipleship, and life concerns. His interesting documentation of this program's success in Christ Church, moreover, includes allusions to two of his own members,

Ron Hamilton and Pauline Hord. Likewise, his comments about the church's ministry with the poor and with the recovering community, in Lecture Three, are grounded in real-life stories such as that of Charles Hall. These stories give special point to Dunnam's plea, quoting John McFarland: "The only way to do evangelism *is just to do it.*"

It is usually the preacher who understands how to use good illustrations appropriately who may be counted upon to succeed as an interpreter of the gospel. What Dr. William Stidger, legendary professor of homiletics at Boston University School of Theology, said years ago is still dependably true: "Illustrations are windows that let the light into the darkened rooms of our thought." One understands better why a person like Maxie Dunnam has been so eminently effective in the proclamation of the Word when he or she has examined carefully the Memphis pastor's illustrative skills.

As the same time, one would be misled if one assumed that these lectures are comprised only of personal stories or anecdotes from the pastorate. Let me pause at this point to pay tribute to the large and fascinating array of important individuals within the larger Christian community to whom Dr. Dunnam repeatedly refers in building the structure for his ideas and emphases. They include such stellar names as Mortimer Arias, William Temple, Lesslie Newbigin, Michael Green, David Lowes Watson, William R. Cannon, John Wesley, Will Campbell, Donald McGavran, David Bosch, and John R.W. Stott.

These sources, some quoted from books they have written and others from addresses heard on various occasions, represent a rich variety of backgrounds and biblical interpretation. They assure the reader of these lectures that the author has taken pains to keep abreast of the best Christian thinking, both past and present. An unusual versatility in the use of illustrative material is evidenced by the fact that Dr. Dunnam moves easily and naturally from reference to some well-known person to the sensitive use of a simple story about a parishioner known only to his or her fellow members and the pastor.

In the final address, Dr. Dunnam sums up the evangelistic ministry of the congregation as a whole by examining and illustrating two key biblical images: the "People of God" and the "Body of Christ." He develops these images in relation to the fellowship and service of the congregation, before returning once again to affirm the place of personal witness. In the end, Dunnam does not want to say that everything the church does is evangelism—that would be "too broad to have driving meaning." He does, however, want to show how "everything the church does should contribute to its evangelistic task."

The 1992 Denman Lectures are vintage Maxie Dunnam. And because of this, they had an eager hearing and, I predict, will enjoy a wide readership.

Earl G. Hunt, Jr.
President, The Foundation for Evangelism
Lake Junaluska, North Carolina
Spring 1992

■

LECTURE 1

_____

Ideas Have Consequences

IDEAS HAVE CONSEQUENCES

Introductory Comments

My wife, Jerry, works hard to keep my feet on the ground. Sometime ago, when some of our children were still at home, we had a siege of the flu. It seemed as though its intent was to attack one person after the other. Everyone in our family had been sick but me when it came time for me to go out of town on a speaking engagement. Jerry and the children were afraid that I would get to a hotel in some strange place and come down with the bug. When I arrived at my hotel and unpacked my bags, I found a note from Jerry in the top of the suitcase. It said, "Cheer up, you have two chances: one of getting the bug, and one of not. And if you get the bug, you have two chances: one of getting sick, and one of not. And if you get sick, you have two chances: one of dying and one of not. And if you die, well, you have two chances."

Well, I have not two, but three chances with you — three lectures on evangelism. These are the Denman Lectures, and you can imagine how tempted one in my place would be to talk about the one in whose honor these lectures were established. Harry Denman personified evangelism. Long before anyone was talking about holistic evangelism, calling into question a narrow definition of evangelism as personal witnessing and/or preaching alone, Harry was practicing holistic evangelism — giving his money away, living the simple life characterized by his one suit and his tiny satchel with an extra shirt and a change of underwear, sharing food with prisoners at Thanksgiving and Christmas — that is, actually going to the jails to spend the holidays there as an act of love and oneness.

Harry talked a lot about evangelism, but he did evangelism more than he talked about it. I pray that would be true of all of us — especially me. If anything I say in these lectures does not sound with integrity, rooted in personal experience, I hope you will call me into question. That's what Harry Denman would insist on: personal involvement and integrity. So, in fear and trembling, I approach my three chances with you, and resist reminiscing about Harry.

1

Definition of Evangelism

Just in case we need some definitions as we begin, I'll make them brief, so that we can be on board together. The word *evangel* is a transliteration of a Greek word which means "good tidings" or "good news."

The New Testament word had two basic uses: one, the good news Jesus proclaimed regarding the kingdom of God; two, the good news *about* Jesus. Jesus both proclaimed the good news of the coming of the kingdom and embodied the good news in his life. Jesus' life, his relations with people, his teaching and preaching, his healings and other miracles, culminating in his death, resurrection, and ascension, revealed and manifested what the kingdom is like. God's sovereign future rule broke into the present in Jesus Christ. Through his love and forgiveness, his ministry of compassion, a new life of freedom and service and an entry into God's kingdom were made available. That ministry was continued by the early Christians "in the name of Jesus Christ." They testified and preached about Jesus Christ. They acted in his name, and those who responded became part of the Christian community.

So, evangelism is the demonstration and proclamation of the gospel. We need to remember that the evangelistic activity of the early church was not limited to preaching. Everything the church was called to be and do in its worship, witness, fellowship, and service was infused and informed by evangelism.

That's my frame of reference in talking about evangelism. But, I don't mean by this that evangelism is everything the church does. That's far too broad to have driving meaning. I do mean that everything the church does should contribute to its evangelistic task. Have you heard Archbishop William Temple's definition of evangelism? "Evangelism is the winning of persons to acknowledge Christ as their Savior and King, so that they may give themselves to his service in the fellowship of the church."[1]

Nothing less than that is evangelism. It's a matter of the Christian community sharing the good news of a Savior with those who do not know him.

So, evangelism is neither Christian proclamation alone, nor Christian presence alone. It is both. For that reason, the primary focus of my lectures is the congregation, the local church. I'm going to talk about theology, about Christian experience, about personal witness, but my focus is the local church. That's the perspective from which I see things.

Word and Deed

I want to begin, however, with that which shapes the church, that is, *the church*, which is God's idea — the continuing incarnation of Christ in the world; but also *our church*, the community of folks who have a specific identity at the corner of Poplar Avenue and Grove Park in Memphis. What shapes *the* church and *our* church and how close are those expressions?

The degree to which *our* church looks like *the* church is dependent upon our whole being — our knowing and our doing — our ideas and how we put those ideas into action.

The relation between what we think and what we do, what we say and how we live, is a very important one for us as Christians. It is also very important in what I want to say to you about evangelism. This relation between word and deed is one that generates a great deal of debate. Some, like the great theologian Karl Barth, have said that evangelism, and thus faith and conversion, can only begin with what we say, what we know, the message preached about Christ. Others, like some contemporary liberation theologians, argue that the words of the evangelist are empty unless they are preceded by deeds which meet the needs and bind up the wounds of those who suffer as they watch and listen.

Much is at stake in this debate. There are dangers on every side. Some fear that if we concentrate on doing deeds of mercy and justice, we will lose the unique focus on Christ which gives us our identity. Others point out that a concern only with preaching and right dogma can render our words empty, meaningless, and irrelevant.

I would not want to try to solve every riddle that resides at the heart of this debate, even if I could. What I do want to do, however, is to recognize the importance of the debate, and I want to address you as pastors and laity of local congregations about where I believe we must take our main bearings. And what I want to begin with in this first lecture is the key and important proposition that *ideas have consequences*.

The Uniqueness of Christ

Will you now at least entertain this dogmatic assertion? *What you think of Jesus Christ will determine what you do about evangelism.*

I believe the greatest *theological* barrier to evangelism today is a diminished belief in the uniqueness of Christ.

I have never felt the church was more on target in its theological emphasis than was the World Methodist Conference meeting in

Singapore in 1991 under the theme, Jesus Christ: God's Saving Word. Sub-themes were: "Jesus Christ, God's Creative Word," "Jesus Christ, God's Incarnate Word," "Jesus Christ, God's Prophetic Word," "Jesus Christ, God's Saving Word" (repeated from overall theme), "Jesus Christ, God's Living Word," and "Jesus Christ, God's Ultimate Word."

What we think of Christ determines what we do about evangelism.

This has been the ongoing debate of the World Council of Churches. In 1968, on the eve of the WCC Assembly, Donald McGavran asked, "Will Upsala betray the 2 billion?" He charged that the World Council had given up concern for the 2 billion people of the earth who had neither heard of Jesus Christ nor had any real chance to believe in him as Lord and Savior.[2]

Philip Potter, who was then secretary of evangelism for the WCC, addressed similar issues in 1967 when he asked the central committee, "Is evangelism at the heart of the life and work of the WCC? What does the WCC mean when it speaks of evangelism? What is to be done to manifest more evidently the central concern of the WCC and its member churches for evangelism?"[3]

Norman Thomas has traced the evolving emphasis on evangelism in the World Council of Churches. The Council inherited a legacy of evangelism as a primary ecumenical concern.

> The focus of the church's mission during the first three decades of this century, David Bosch declares, was on *evangelism*. Thereafter from Tambaram (1938) to New Delhi (1961) the *church* was the primary focus. The Constitution of the WCC since its founding in 1948 had included the function and purpose "to support the churches in their worldwide missionary and evangelistic tasks." A Secretariat for evangelism was set up in 1949. After New Delhi, however, the *world* was emphasized increasingly as the primary focus of God's concern, with salvation understood as including both personal and social liberation.[4]

Continuing for the moment to follow Thomas' analysis, we should note that evangelism regained a central place at the WCC's Fifth Assembly in Nairobi in 1975. This was evident both in Section I entitled, "Confessing Christ Today," and in Bishop Mortimer Arias' plenary address entitled, "That the World May Believe." Arias urged that evangelism is an "essential," "primary," "normal," "permanent," and "costly" task of the church. John Stott, an Anglican delegate and chief architect of the Lausanne Covenant (1974), responded by calling the WCC to recover five emphases:

(1) A recognition of the lostness of humanity

(2) Confidence in the gospel
(3) Conviction about the uniqueness of Christ
(4) A sense of urgency about evangelism
(5) A personal experience of Jesus Christ

"In the public discussion," according to Thomas, "Bishop Arias was quite happy with Stott's last four points, only preferring to proceed from the love of God rather than from the lostness of humanity."[5]

Ideas do have consequences. Wasn't Arias begging the question? Whether you proceed from the point of the love of God, or from the lostness of humanity, the central issue is the uniqueness of Jesus Christ. He is the incarnate love of God offered as God's saving grace for lost humanity. *What we think about Jesus Christ determines what we do about evangelism.*

And that raises, of course, the question of our confidence in the gospel. Go back to Archbishop Temple's definition of evangelism: *"Evangelism is the winning of persons to acknowledge Christ as their Savior and King, so that they may give themselves to his service in the fellowship of the church."*

You can't have a definition of evangelism like that, much less practice it, without confidence in the gospel. The apostles preached the gospel, in season and out, because they believed in Christ. They applied the great christological titles to him precisely in order to recognize his unique person and work. He is Messiah, Son of Man, High Priest, Prophet, King, Lord, Savior, and Son of God. As if that were not enough, the New Testament proceeds to address Jesus as the "Word of God," and finally as "God." Jesus is at the heart of the New Testament message.

Carl Braaten echoes the scriptural sense of urgency about the claim to Christ's uniqueness.

The Gospel is the good news of what God has done to death in raising Jesus from the grave; that is the heart of the message of the Apostles . . . "Christ is risen!" Death has been conquered at Easter and a new ruler has been enthroned in the world. "Christ is King." The effect of this event is absolutely decisive, uniquely authoritative, and universally valid. As Matthew 28:18-20 states the matter: "All authority" has been given to Christ; "all nations" are to be made disciples and baptized in the name of the Triune God; they are to be taught "all that I have commanded you;" and Christ promises to be with his followers "always to the close of the age."[6]

Ideas have consequences. If we don't have confidence in the gospel, if we're not solidly convicted about the uniqueness of Christ, it is not likely that evangelism will have much priority in our personal ministry and/or in our church. What we think of Christ determines what we do about evangelism.

The Nature of Grace

Move to another theological issue, a big idea with enormous consequences: *what we think about grace.* Grace is at the heart of the gospel — amazing grace. What we think about grace shapes our evangelistic message and determines our evangelistic urgency.

The apostle John captured it in this encompassing word: "For God so loved the world that he gave his only Son, so that everyone who believes in him may not perish but may have eternal life. Indeed, God did not send the Son into the world to condemn the world, but in order that the world might be saved through him" (John 3:16-17).

And this is what Paul argued about so convincingly with the Romans: "Since all have sinned and fall short of the glory of God; they are now justified by his grace as a gift, through the redemption that is in Christ Jesus, whom God put forward as a sacrifice of atonement by his blood, effective through faith" (Romans 8:23-25).

John Wesley did a great service and provided a distinctive emphasis by talking about grace impinging upon us and working in three specific ways: prevenient grace, justifying grace, and sanctifying grace. Prevenient grace is the grace of God going before us, pulling us, wooing us, seeking to open our minds and hearts, and eventually giving us faith. Justifying grace is the forgiving love of God, freely given to us, reconciling us, putting us right with God, making Christ, who knew no sin, to be sin on our behalf. Sanctifying grace is the work and Spirit of Christ within us, restoring the broken image, completing the salvation which was begun in justification, and bringing us to complete newness of life and perfection in love.

Certainly our understanding and experience of grace impacts our witness and determines in large part the way we do evangelism. If we believe that God loves us and all people, seeking us and them before we seek God, we can witness with confidence, but also in humility, knowing that we cannot limit the saving love of God, and that we don't do the saving work — God does.

We need to remember that Wesley sounded the note of grace strongly in opposition to a doctrine of predestination. Whether the rigid, double predestination idea — that some are damned to hell while others are elected to heaven — or another variation on that theme, the doctrine of predestination has as its center an understanding of grace being limited. For Wesley, grace is not limited — it is universal. It is "free in all, and free for all." Bishop William R. Cannon makes the case.

> To be sure, it is free to all in the sense that it is given without price, that it does not demand anything of us before it is bestowed, and that it flows from the mercy of God. But note the change. Grace is free for all. It is not free only for those whom God has ordained to life, but it is like the air we breathe, or the wind that blows in our faces; it is for everyone who dwells upon the face of the earth.[7]

Now that doesn't mean that all persons receive this grace, or that they deliberately appropriate it, or respond to it for their salvation. They don't. That is the reason Wesley sounded so clearly the note of repentance. God's prevenient grace works in our lives to lead us to repentance which is a necessary response for salvation. Repentance is both a step and an ongoing response. God's grace is universal, but prevenient grace is not sufficient for salvation. A person may suppress or ignore this grace. If so, scripture warns that we may experience hardness of heart, so that the stirrings of the Spirit within will go unheeded.

This raises one of the thorniest issues in theology today — the issue of universal grace and universal salvation. There are two prongs to the issue. One prong is the trend in both Protestant and Catholic theology that makes Christ "small and unimportant." The uniqueness of Christ as God's source of salvation is under attack.

Listen to Carl Braaten: "The christocentric emphasis is under attack, at least among the deans of modern liberal Protestant and Catholic progressive theology. Our biblical evangelical reformation christology is too exclusivistic [they say]. . . . On account of historical relativity and religious pluralism, many are challenging the place of Christ as the goal of things. Is Christ really that final, definitive and normative?"[8]

Braaten is so bold as to identify some of the leaders of this theological movement that diminishes the uniqueness of Christ.

> John Hick represents a liberal Protestant view which allows Christians to hold to Christ as their unique Savior without necessarily claiming as much for others. Christ may be my personal Lord and Savior, but this does not mean that he is the only Savior or the only Lord for all other religions. To hold Christ as the final and normative Word of God is branded as "theological fundamentalism." There is room, after all, for other savior figures in other religions, at least enough to go around for everybody. To be sure, Jesus is one of the ways in which God meets the world of human experience,

but it is arrogant bigotry to claim that Jesus is God's unique way of dealing with the salvation of the world.

Other voices in modern theology like Tom Driver, RoseMary Ruether, and Dorothee Sölle are claiming that the uniqueness, normativity, and finality of Jesus Christ account for the sins of Christianity, its sexism, racism, and anti-Semitism. The scandal of particularity that insists on a once-and-for-all Christ is supposedly the breeding ground of intolerance, supremacy, imperialism, and what these theologians call "Christofascism." . . . What these theologians are asking for is a "paradigm shift" from a theology wherein Christ is the center to one in which he is one of the satellites in a galaxy of religious superstars.[9]

Braaten makes a powerful and convincing case against the diminishing of the uniqueness of Christ. Ironically, however, he does so to undergird what seems to be his own commitment to universal salvation. And that's the other prong of this thorny issue of universal grace and universal salvation.

The first prong makes Christ "small and unimportant." The second prong does not diminish the uniqueness of Christ, but insists that his saving grace will work universally, and eventually all will come into God's kingdom through the work of Christ.

Braaten's article is similar in this regard to the powerful yet flawed argument of David Lowes Watson in *God Does Not Foreclose*. What a marvelous title! I found myself, almost on every page of this book, saying "Yeah!" "Right on!" "That's right!" Listen to Watson:

In Christ we have the assurance that God wants all people to be part of the heavenly family, taking full advantage of their new birth right. This is the work of grace that transcends the heights and plumbs the depth of our being as we never thought possible. Not only are we forgiven all that separates us from God, past, present, or future, and whether or not we are to blame. We are reconciled to God in a new relationship, which can best be described in two words: Welcome Home![10]

We can shout Amen to that, can't we?
    Listen again:

When we look at the cross, and remember our own spiritual homecoming, we realize how much God was willing to risk, and continues to risk, to have us back home. For God will always give us the freedom to accept this gracious invitation, or refuse it. We can all recall what it is like to be rejected by someone, even by a stranger; and much worse, the shock and the pain of rejection by a friend, a spouse, a daughter, or a son. We can then begin to sense the depth of God's anguish throughout human history. Not one prodigal, but millions of daughters and sons across the centuries have lived their lives away from their true home. Alienated from their true family, they have suffered from the ravages of human sin, either as sinners, or as those who are sinned against. It is incalculable how much grief and torment this has heaped on a God who is more loving and protective than any human mother, more trustworthy and concerned than any earthly father. This is why our surrender to God's grace, our acceptance of God's invitation to come home, is such an overwhelmingly joyous occasion.[11]

Another loud Amen!

That's the way I read the book — saying "Yeah" and "Amen" throughout the whole thing; except, and this is the big except, while I agreed with maybe 90 percent of both Braaten's article and Watson's book, the little I disagreed with makes all the difference in the world in our thinking about and doing the work of evangelism. The point at which I disagree is their big point — and the big point of those who hold to a universal *accomplished* salvation: God does not foreclose on sinners. Watson quotes these lines from Braaten:

> The good news is that all people have been united with God in Christ. One chief difference between the Christian and the non-Christian is that the one knows and the other does not yet know.[12]

My question is, is that the chief difference? Are all persons united with God in Christ, and some of us who call ourselves Christians know it, but others who don't know it are guaranteed salvation as well? This seems to me to be begging the question. Listen again to Braaten:

> The threat of eternal condemnation is real for all people. Nevertheless, there is no basis to assert that God will necessarily in the end actualize this possibility. Christians may hope and pray that all might be saved, that the distinction between those who already believe and those who do not yet believe will ultimately be destroyed by the Word of God who "is able from these stones to raise up children to Abraham" (Matthew 3:9).[13]

So Braaten at least draws back from asserting that God will actualize the possibility of eternal salvation for everyone.

Of course, we can hope and pray — and as Christians we will hope and pray for the redemption of all humankind. But I for one will continue to be challenged by Jesus' parable of the last judgment, and the awful possibility that I may be among those who did not serve "the least of these" and will hear that awful verdict: "these will go away into eternal punishment, but the righteous into eternal life" (Matthew 25:46). I will continue to seek to stay alive and awake so that I will not hear as Jesus said in his parable of the bridesmaids: "The door is shut." And this awareness will continue to press upon me the urgency of sharing the news of God's love in Christ with those who have yet to hear, and those who have so far rejected or resisted grace.

Ideas have consequences. What we think about Jesus determines what we do about evangelism. And what we do about evangelism is shaped by what we think about grace.

What I have said thus far should make it clear, at least implicitly, that I am not eager to draw conclusions about the ultimate salvific status of others. To proclaim the uniqueness of Christ, and the reality of divine judgment, is not one and the same with pronouncing our own judgment forthwith. In the Wesleyan tradition, the danger of rejecting grace is always counterbalanced by the wonder of what can happen in our lives when we accept and cooperate with it. Therefore, I wonder if you can entertain my putting my first dogmatic assertion in a slightly different way? What you think Jesus can do for a person will determine what you do about evangelism.

What Christ Can Do

I began the actual writing of these lectures on October 29, 1991. I had set aside that week, October 28 to November 3, for a study leave. My time was shortened by two days because of the funeral of my brother-in-law, Randy Morris. Randy was forty-three years old and had fought a courageous battle with cancer. Two years ago my wife, Jerry, gave him a bone marrow transplant, and it looked like Randy was going to make it. But he didn't. So my study leave, and the beginning of actual writing of these lectures, was delayed by Randy's funeral.

What a funeral it was! What a celebration. Randy had planned it, selecting the scriptures, hymns, and prayer. I've never experienced more moving worship.

People spoke the words of the liturgy with power and conviction. They sang strongly and joyfully. Why and how? They knew Randy. They knew what Christ had done in Randy's life.

Let me tell you about Randy.

Early on in his illness, after the first round of chemotherapy, Randy went into remission and everything looked good. Then it struck again. We who have not experienced it can only faintly imagine the trauma of recurring malignancy.

I had sent Randy some sermons I had preached on the Psalms. One of them was a theme from Psalm 56, "Put thou my tears in thy bottle." In my sermon, I had affirmed that God *not only knows* our tossings and turnings, *God cares.* Randy responded with a beautiful witness about trust. He wrote me a letter.

I have grown to love the Psalms during this past year. It is true that God does know of all our tossings.

And now I will share with you a prayer experience that proves this to me. It was a major experience with Jesus. Father Rick says I have been touched in a way few people ever experience.

For several years I have prepared for prayer by going through a total relaxation phase to release my body and mind for prayer. After a few moments I travel in my mind to a place in the north Georgia mountains where I used to go on camping trips. There I have built an open structure, a gazebo, where I go to talk with Jesus. Normally I go in and call for Jesus and he comes. We visit, and usually I give him my prayers of thanksgiving and intercessions. It's a conversational sort of setting.

In late August, I was completely demoralized with the recurrence of the lymphoma. I was an emotional wreck; I went into prayer. Everything went on as normal until Jesus came to the door of the gazebo. At that moment a completely unthought-of event happened that shook me to tears. I became like a camera recording the event. A little boy, me, when I was about five years old, ran up to Jesus and hugged him. He picked me up and carried me to a seat and held me in his arms. He hugged me. I didn't say anything, but he knew my "tossings." He knew I was frightened. There were no answers and the future seemed so dim. As he hugged me he said, "Trust me. Trust me."

It was real, a personal miracle. He held me for a long time that night, until he knew I understood what he meant. I've told just a few people about this, and every time I tell it, even as I type this for you, tears come to my eyes; and the feeling I experienced that night renews itself in me. Rick said that feeling is "the same reason Moses couldn't look God in the face and why we remove our shoes (when we stand) on holy ground." And now I know that experience, too. We must trust Jesus as a child trusts — totally.

Because of this, whatever turns out to be the ultimate result of this disease, it's not the burden it was before. He made no promise, nor did he reveal the future, but he provided the format for living out the rest of my life with just two words . . . Trust me."[14]

Well, Randy did that — from that point on. He *trusted* Jesus. The difference it made in his life, the power of his witness, the number of people he ministered to, all combined to tell a phenomenal story of what Christ can do for a person.

In one of his last letters to me, when complete physical healing seemed to be taking place, he said:

> But the healing will be deeper than that [i.e., physical healing]. There will be full reconciliation within my spirit and soul such as I have never enjoyed before. I truly feel the words written in The Book of Common Prayer about reconciliation: "Now there is rejoicing in heaven; for you were lost, and are found; you were dead, and are now alive in Christ Jesus our Lord. Go in peace. The Lord has put away all your sins. Thanks be to God"[15]

As a result of Randy's witness, many people have grown in their own relationship with Christ, and in their desire to share the joy of this relationship with others. What you think Christ can do for a person will determine what you do about evangelism.

Let me rehearse. The big point of this lecture is that ideas have consequences. I have affirmed three things:

(1) *What you think about Christ determines what you do about evangelism.* If we don't have confidence in the gospel, and if we are not solidly convicted about the uniqueness of Christ, it is not likely that evangelism will have much priority in our personal ministry and/or in our church.

(2) *What we do about evangelism is shaped by what we think about grace.* If we think that grace is limited, or that all people are automatically saved, we will not be likely to proclaim the message of grace with any urgency to all people. If, on the other hand, we realize that grace is unlimited, and that salvation can be rejected, we will share urgently and with all.

(3) *What you think Jesus can do for a person will determine what you do about evangelism.* Remembering a story like Randy's, or our own story, is one of the greatest motivations possible to share the good news with others.

The big idea that has phenomenal consequences is what we think about the uniqueness of Jesus.

The Power of the Holy Spirit

But now, I must turn our discussion in a new direction. Actually, it is not a new direction, but the other side of the coin of the relation between word and deed with which we began. If ideas have consequences, it is also true that *consequences shape ideas*; that is, what we do in evangelizing (our being, our behavior, how we conduct ourselves in the Spirit) can and does have a powerful bearing on what we say, what we believe, and how what we say we believe is heard by those who watch and listen.

In one sense, for the remainder of this lecture and the next two, I will be dealing with this other angle, this flip-side of the theme that ideas have consequences. We shall not deny or contradict our first theme, but we shall look at it the other way around.

Consider a fourth proposition, only this proposition moves us beyond the level of assertion. It moves us beyond the level of evangelistic content per se, to the level of encounter and trust. The proposition is this: What you *think* about evangelism won't matter much unless the Holy Spirit empowers you.

At the beginning of his ministry, Jesus gave us the charter of the kingdom when he announced his mission:

> The Spirit of the Lord is upon me, because he has anointed me to bring good news to the poor. He has sent me to proclaim release to the captives and recovery of sight to the blind, to let the oppressed go free, to proclaim the year of the Lord's favor (Luke 4:18-19).

At the close of his ministry, he commissioned us for kingdom work:

> And Jesus came and said to them, "All authority in heaven and on earth has been given to me. Go therefore and make disciples of all nations, baptizing them in the name of the Father and of the Son and of the Holy Spirit, and teaching them to obey everything that I have commanded you. And remember, I am with you always, to the end of the age" (Matthew 28:19-20).

At the center of his charter and his commission for the kingdom is the Holy Spirit: "The Spirit of the Lord is upon me . . . Go . . .make disciples . . . baptizing them in the name of the Father and of the Son and of the Holy Spirit."

Not only are the charter and the commission of the kingdom centered in the Spirit, his commitment to provide us power is Spirit-centered. Listen to Acts 1:6-8:

So when they had come together, they asked him, "Lord, is this the time when you will restore the kingdom to Israel?" He replied, "It is not for you to know the times or periods that the Father has set by his own authority. But you will receive power when the Holy Spirit has come upon you; and you will be my witnesses in Jerusalem, in all Judea and Samaria, and to the ends of the earth."

So, according to Jesus, at the heart of kingdom business is evangelism, and the power source of evangelism is the Holy Spirit. What you think about evangelism will not matter much unless the Holy Spirit empowers your effort.

Notice two things that this implies. It implies, first, that evangelism and the Holy Spirit go together. We cannot do evangelism effectively without the power and presence of the Holy Spirit. Likewise, if we are following the Spirit, we will be evangelizing — not just talking about it, but doing it. Michael Green has noted this bond as a hallmark of the New Testament church, and a sign of poverty in the experience of the church today. He asks penetrating questions:

Could it be that we know so little of the Spirit in any powerful way because we care so little for evangelism? Equally, that we know so little of evangelism in any powerful way because we know so little of the Spirit? These two God has joined together, and we cannot put them asunder. No evangelism, no Holy Spirit: No Holy Spirit, no evangelism. There is a vital link between them: and that explains a good deal of the powerlessness in the modern church.[16]

So we need to remember, what we think about evangelism won't matter much unless the Holy Spirit empowers our efforts.

The second truth this implies is that if the power to evangelize comes from the Holy Spirit, so does the result. We must never forget that we evangelize, but the Holy Spirit converts. Our programs and models and styles of evangelism must be shaped by this truth, this trust. Not only so, it is only as we remember this that we will remain faithful to the task. You see, if we think that we convert, then our doing evangelism would be dependent upon how we measure success, and on whether we are successful or not. But success is not an issue in evangelism. We're called to evangelize — that is, to share the witness of Jesus Christ — knowing that the Spirit converts. If anyone is successful in evangelism, it is the Holy Spirit. Albert Outler stated this point clearly:

The chief dynamic of valid evangelism is the power and prevenience of the Holy Spirit. In all we say and do, we presuppose that the

Holy Spirit is already there, awakening faith, preparing the heart and mind and will. This does not reduce the human share in the process to insignificance, but it does set up priorities between God's untrammelled freedom and initiative and human responsibility (which is to say, the human ability to respond!).[17]

But now this casts some additional light on our earlier discussions about the uniqueness of Christ, and the universal *offer* of salvation. Though we believe that Christ is the unique Savior of the world, and that grace — though offered universally — must still be accepted and received to become efficacious, this does not put us in control of the ways of the Spirit in the lives of other people. The timetable of salvation belongs to the Spirit. We cannot presume to predict or pronounce divine judgment upon other souls.

What do we say about those throughout history and alive in the world today who have never heard the gospel of Jesus Christ? "God's grace is great; the Spirit discerns the heart" (Romans 2:14-16). What do we say about those who have heard and rejected? "God's grace is great; the Spirit is not through with any of us yet." What do we say about those who appear to have taken their rejection of Christ with them to the grave? "God's grace is great; Lord, have mercy; there but for grace go I." None of this requires that we reject the uniqueness of Christ, the universal offer of salvation, or the reality of divine judgment. Nor does it require that we take the mantle of judgment unto ourselves. The power and motive for evangelism remain fully intact.

Now this turn of ideas may leave you wondering. I began this lecture with the dogmatic assertion that ideas have consequences; what you think about Jesus, and about grace, and about what Jesus can do for a person, has everything to do with how you do evangelism. And now I am saying that what you think about evangelism, about all of these things, will not matter much unless the Holy Spirit empowers you. In fact, we may be perfectly correct in what we think and yet miss the Spirit and power of evangelism altogether.

In the next two lectures, I will pursue in more detail the implications of this final point: what it means to evangelize in the power (and on the timetable of) the Holy Spirit. For now, let me sum up the heart of this first lecture by returning to the witness of Randy's funeral.

After the interment, we returned to his little Episcopal church for food and fellowship. The affirmation of Randy's faith and the witness of people whose lives he had touched was causing me to overflow with joy.

I was walking down the hallway and came to a bulletin board. "Evangelism" was written in big letters across the top, so I stopped to look at what Episcopalians were doing about evangelism. There were a lot of announcements, many of which didn't seem to me to have much to do with evangelism. But one item did. It was a graphic poster which made this statement: "If you have everything but don't have Jesus, you have nothing. If you have nothing, but have Jesus, you have everything."

My joy was full. I thanked God for Randy. He had witnessed to me in life. He had witnessed to me in death. And now his Episcopal church was telling this Methodist preacher what evangelism is all about. If you have everything and don't have Jesus, you have nothing. If you have nothing but have Jesus, you have everything.

Discipleship Evangelism

■

DISCIPLESHIP EVANGELISM

■

Introductory Comments

I trembled when I thought of it, and began preparation. How presumptuous of me to accept the invitation to deliver the Denman Lectures on Evangelism. What do I know about evangelism?

What makes me tremble now, even after the lectures are over, is that you rather than I may be shaping the question differently: "What does he know about evangelism?"

My only credential is that I'm seeking to do evangelism in the local church. Sometimes in that setting we don't do according to what we know, and that's a sin. Isn't that scriptural? "Anyone, then, who knows the right thing to do and fails to do it, commits sins" (James 4:17).

But also, in the local church setting, we sometimes do, but we don't reflect on our doing. Now, that may not be a sin like failing to do what we know, but it does limit our effectiveness. When we don't reflect on what we're doing, we fail to test our theories and practices. Also, for persons doing evangelism in the local church setting, the failure to reflect, and to share our reflections with each other, limits the possibility of church renewal and a resurgence of church growth.

The Importance of Congregations

Maybe that's what those who invited me to deliver these lectures had in mind. Or, maybe they perceived two years ago when they invited me what John Robert McFarland wrote about in his article in *The Christian Century* October 23, 1991. He titled his article "What's Wrong With the 'What's Wrong' Books?" I agree with McFarland:

In the past few years we've been subjected to dozens of 'What's-wrong-with-the-mainline' books. They claim to know why our churches are declining, and what to do about that decline. They have not been helpful, however, because they build on inadequate, if not false, premises.[1]

McFarland lists what's wrong with the what's wrong books. I abbreviate and add to his points.

First, these books "do not take the local parish seriously."

At some point in the ecclesiastical journey of the mainline churches, some people forgot that the basic unit of the whole church is the local congregation. It's quite understandable for people to consider general assemblies, [judicatories,] conferences, publication boards, executives, and agencies as "the denomination." These are the connecting links within a denomination. The whole church, however, is primarily local, not denominational. The congregations together are the denomination. Therefore, problems of decline must be addressed at the local level [, or they cannot be addressed at all.][2]

Second, the "What's Wrong" books are often misguided "in placing blame and in finding solutions. Because some don't take the local parish seriously, they assume that denominational leaders have done, thought or said something that has caused the mainline decline"; or that denominational leaders are the ones to whom we should primarily look to find solutions. Denominational structures can and often do contribute to a mentality that wittingly or unwittingly ignores the local congregation; "but the source of the problem, and thus the source of the solution, is the local congregation."[3] McFarland continues:

Most finger-pointers look for bogeymen (and bogeywomen) in bureaucracies and seminaries. They [rarely] consider looking at parish lay leaders, board chairpeople, greeters or ushers. I am not suggesting that we use parish leaders and members as scapegoats for mainline sins. The parish is, however, where the action is. It is useless to blame denominational structures. . . .[4]

If the structures ignore the local congregations, they will not ultimately affect anything, anyway. What we need, by contrast, is a renewed confidence in the role of the local congregation, and a renewed call to our denominational structures to get in touch with this confidence as well.

Third, some of the "What's Wrong" books imply that "parish pastors are part of the problem, but not part of the solution." McFarland states the issue forcefully:

If we do not take local churches seriously, we're not likely to take their pastors seriously, either. The "What's Wrong" books find much that's wrong with pastors, from their education to their lack of a sacrificial or evangelistic spirit. They don't believe, however, that pastors could help reverse the mainline's downward trends. For instance, when the whole church tries to do something about numerical decline it hires consultants who are not pastors. But we already have in place the best church growth consultant network available: pastors. This group has more members, and thus more potential, than all the other ordained ministry groups in a denomination — chaplains, consultants, editors, teachers — put together. But who writes the articles in almost any denominational magazine for pastors? Professors, executives and other non-parish ministers write eighty percent of them. And these same folk usually head continuing-education conferences for pastors. Where are the parish ministers? If the congregation is the basic and one indispensable unit of the whole church, however, and mainline problems are actually congregational rather than denominational, we are going to have to rely on pastors to help solve our problems. That's not likely to happen if people continue to act as though pastors create but cannot solve problems.[5]

So here I am — a pastor in a local church — believing that if the problems are in the local church, then the solutions must be there as well. There are signs in The United Methodist Church that sensitivity between denominational structures and local congregations is on the rise. Thank God for our 500 Growth Plus Consultants in United Methodism who are pastors who have been trained by the Section on Evangelism of the General Board of Discipleship to help local congregations. Thank God also for the signs we have in publications such as *Vision 2000* by Joe Harding and Ralph Mohney, and *Every Member in Ministry* by John Ed Mathison, that our denominational publishers are seeking the wisdom of veteran pastors and congregations as the model for renewal. These signs of encouragement and hope give me renewed confidence, in these lectures, to share my personal convictions as a pastor and to reflect on why and how the congregation I seek to lead does its ministry.

Therefore, in this lecture, I'm looking at the nature of evangelism. In the next, we will look at the nature of the church. I struggled with which should come first and still cannot be sure the order is right. Perhaps like the chicken and the egg, the best thing to say is that we cannot have one without the other.

Evangelism and Discipleship

Georgia Harkness once said, "We must rescue evangelism from the red-light district of the ecclesiastical community." Well, that's putting it pretty straight. Evangelism has been prostituted for money and personal gain. That's all the more reason we need to remind ourselves that the focus of evangelism must be the local congregation, not primarily the streetcorner, the storefront, or the television. And we can't talk about local church evangelism without talking about evangelizing the local church.

In his parting word to the disciples, Jesus said, "You will be my witnesses in Jerusalem, in all Judea and Samaria, and to the ends of the earth" (Acts 1:8).

He spoke this word to the persons he had chosen, trained, tested, and nurtured. His charge to them was not a heavy command, "you ought to" or "you must"; not even "you should." It was a simple statement of fact. "You will be my witnesses."

In another setting, Jesus gave his call to the early church: "Go therefore and make disciples of all nations, baptizing them in the name of the Father and of the Son and of the Holy Spirit, . . . and remember, I am with you always, to the end of the age" (Matthew 28:19-20). There was no room for confusion about direction in this explicit instruction of our Lord. Spreading the gospel was to be top priority. No Christian was exempted from the task of disciple-making, and no aspect of life was excluded.

While the so-called great commission has been used as a foundation in evangelistic literature, and a challenge to churches to fulfill their missionary and evangelistic responsibility, it is more than that. It is a definition of the nature of mission itself. The resurrected Lord calls his disciples to "make disciples of all nations . . . baptizing and teaching them."

In the past couple of decades, there has been a renewed emphasis on discipleship in evangelism. One of the chief promoters of this emphasis, according to Mortimer Arias, has been the Church Growth school under the leadership of Donald McGavran; so much so that they have coined the term *discipling* as the verbal form to describe the evangelistic task. According to Arias, " 'Making disciples' is for [McGavran] the specific evangelistic mission, and 'teaching and baptizing' are left to other ministries in the church, and for a later stage in the life of the convert or disciple."[6]

Lesslie Newbigin, as Arias also notes, has charged that "McGavran's exegesis of the text will not stand scrutiny. It is clear in the original Greek that 'disciple the nations' is the main verb, and that 'baptizing and teaching' are adverbial clauses defining what 'discipling' is."[7]

Thus, while we can agree with McGavran that discipling is the heart of evangelism, we can also agree with Newbigin (against McGavran) that discipling (and thus evangelism) includes "baptizing and teaching."

This was our Lord's definition. All too often, however, it has not been the practice of these who claim to evangelize. The evangelism of the electronic church, for example, does not seem to be too concerned about making disciples. Further, I doubt if these "trans-national corporations of evangelism," as Mortimer Arias calls them, are taking seriously the call to make disciples which in Jesus' own words means "teaching them to observe all things I have commanded you."

We don't have time to explore in depth all of what this means, but we can at least register the direction of what is implied for the local church. The Great Commission sends us back to *everything* Jesus taught. Certainly if we wanted a summary of the content of everything Jesus taught, it would be Jesus' own summary of the law and the prophets and the great commandment: "You shall love the Lord your God with all your heart, and with all your soul, and with all your mind" (Matthew 22:37).

So, John R. W. Stott, the British evangelical leader was right when he declared at the 1974 Lausanne Conference on World Evangelization: "There is no Great Commission without the Great Commandment."[8] We can't talk about evangelism in and through the local church without talking about discipleship. And we can't talk about discipleship without talking about evangelism.

I don't mean that this is easy and goes forward without any hitches or without opposition. The tension between evangelism and disciple-making is still there, I think, in most congregations. It is certainly present in mine. I have members in my church whose zeal for evangelism is an escape from Christ's call to social righteousness and engagement with justice issues. More often than not, they are not conscious of the fact that they are using evangelistic zeal as a diversion, an escape.

On the other hand, I have members whose personal faith and religious feelings are obviously so limited and unsatisfying that they throw themselves into mission and social action. They are quick to condemn personal witness and a passion for souls as irrelevant. They give themselves with passion to causes and leave unfulfilled the spiritual longings of their lives.

For my part, I keep trying to preach sermons that defy this schizoid understanding of the gospel: As Paul suggested in his exasperated question in 1 Corinthians 1:13: "Is Christ divided?" I continue to underscore the call of Jesus, "Go into all the world and preclaim the good news to the whole creation" (Mark 16:15), and his insistence that "repentance and forgiveness of sins is to be proclaimed in his name to all nations" (Luke 24:47). Obedience to this call of Jesus to witness, to evangelize, is a test of loyalty to him.

But I do not let the congregation forget that Jesus also gave us the supreme test just before his crucifixion. He pictured the last judgment as a time when his true disciples would be separated from the unfaithful. He made one distinction between the faithful and the unfaithful. The true disciples would be those who have carried out his great commission to care for the distressed (Matthew 25: 31-46): "Just as you did it to one of the least of these who are members of my family, you did it to me."

> [Jesus'] final commandment to evangelize never mentioned ministering to the hungry, the sick, or the imprisoned; but his test of true discipleship never referred to evangelizing. Did Jesus not know his own mind? But there is no contradiction here. There is just one commandment by which all will be tested — the commandment to care for those in need. [There is no great commission without the great commandment.] Looking out over the city in all its misery, it was *physical suffering* that Jesus mentioned. At his departure into the heavenly glory, it was spiritual needs of which He spoke. Each implies the other. Those are the twin aspects of the Gospel. *(emphasis added)* [9]

This, according to George Sweazey, is why so much talk about a polarization between personal evangelism and the social gospel is absurd. The church was born out of concern for the whole person, the whole world, the whole gospel. We are "not allowed to choose whether to be an evangelistic or a social gospel Christian. The world can never have enough of either." [10]

But not only do I keep preaching this non-schizoid understanding of the gospel, I keep reminding my congregation that Methodism at its best has always held these two aspects of the gospel together. John Wesley said, "The Gospel of Christ knows of no religion but social; no holiness but social holiness." [11] It doesn't hurt us to be redundant and keep telling the folks that historians such as Halévy, Green, Lecky, and Trevelyan, believed that England escaped a revolution like that in France only because of the Wesleyan combination of evangelism and social action. [12] The English trade union movement started in Methodist meeting houses. The Wesleyan revival roused concern for public health, hospital care, prison reform, public education, and the abolition of slavery.

So the local church needs to be evangelized to evangelize. We need to be deliberate in our churches in "making disciples" who will in turn "make disciples." We must nurture and cherish the bond between word and deed, ideas and consequences, beliefs and actions. And the primary place where this kind of evangelizing can and must take place is the local congregation.

Sometime ago, I was driving on Poplar Avenue, a main street in Memphis on which our church is located. The car ahead of me had a bumper sticker. The bumper sticker is a way for a lot of people to sow whatever seeds they want to sow in the minds of other people. Also, it is one of our dominant means of communication, to say to the world around us that we'd "rather be sailing," or that we "love our dog." When I got close enough to the car ahead of me to read the bumper sticker, I saw, in big letters, "I am a generic Christian." Well, that attracted me. I wanted to know what that meant. So, I got closer to the car, knowing that there were some smaller letters written beneath those large ones. I got dangerously close to the back of the car to read the words: "Ask me what I mean." Well, that intrigued me even more.

I suppose my interest was whetted further by the fact that the car on which that bumper sticker was displayed was a $65,000 Mercedes. I wondered how any driver of a Mercedes could be considered a generic anything. The car turned into the carwash. I had no intention of getting a car wash that day, but my interest had so peaked that I couldn't pass it up. So I turned in to get my car washed also — but really to engage that fellow in conversation.

He told me that, while he was a member of a local congregation in our city, he was so tired of the denominational emphasis in so many churches that he wanted to proclaim a different kind of message — that the important message was to be Christian in the generic sense, not a "brand-name Christian." Well, he had a point.

But I wonder if, on the other hand, we don't have too many generic Christians and not enough disciples. Sometimes the reaction to "denominationalism" can become an excuse for refusing to be involved in any actual congregation. Still, to merit the faithfulness of erstwhile generic Christians, congregations must be prepared to get deeply and truly involved in the privilege and challenge of making disciples.

Design for Discipleship

Being convicted of this, a few years ago, we developed in our church what we call a "Design for Discipleship." We came to an awareness that much of what we did in our programming for the church was episodic. We would do a preaching mission now, a mini-conference on another occasion, a celebration, a Bible or missions conference; and on and on it would go. Different program offerings — for the most part, episodic through the year. Seemingly, no connecting point. No underlying purpose for them. So, we came up with a "Design for Discipleship." We wanted to try in our own feeble way to move people along the road of discipleship. For instance, if they were at what they would think of as Point C, maybe we could get them to Point H — just to move them along in some deliberate way in their discipleship growth.

The driving notion for our design was this: "That Christians might be reasonably informed, reasonably inspired, and reasonably equipped." Let me briefly describe that design for you. It has four tracks:

- Spiritual Discipline and Growth
- Bible and Theology
- Applied Discipleship
- Life Concerns.

On the Spiritual Discipline and Growth track, we have ongoing support growth groups, but also twice a year, we offer an invitation to the entire membership to become part of an eight-week growth group experiment. Prayer, Bible study, and sharing are the ingredients of all of these. Once a year, one of these growth group experiments will have a mission theme as its study resource.

On the Bible and Theology track, we offer Disciple Bible Study (information on enrollment available from Cokesbury bookstores), a Bible study every Wednesday night, and twice a year I teach a five- or six-week course on Wesleyan theology, using my book, *Going on to Salvation* (Discipleship Resources, order no. DR100B).

On the Applied Discipleship track, we offer training in faith-sharing, using Eddie Fox and George Morris' book *Faith-Sharing* (Discipleship Resources, order no. DR039B) — and we'll probably use their new book, *Let the Redeemed of the Lord Say So* (available from Abingdon Press). We train people in caregiving for the elderly and hospitalized. We train persons in ministry to teenagers and also in general parenting skills. On this track we also look at pressing social issues that call for our witness, such as housing concerns in our city.

The fourth track, Life Concerns, includes grief support groups, divorce recovery, marriage enrichment, recovery from addiction, and other life concerns.

Most of this work, apart from Sunday school and the growth groups, is done on Wednesday night. Nine months out of the year, we have supper at the church every week with multiple study opportunities offered. Our hope is that evangelism and making disciples will flow out of the same commitment: our response to the Great Commission and the Great Commandment. There is no Great Commission without the Great Commandment.

Let me share with you the witness of one person who has responded to this design. Ron Hamilton gave this witness in our worship services on October 6, 1991. Ron chose his theme as part of our stewardship emphasis: "I am excited about Christ United Methodist Church because it is challenging me to grow." Listen to him:

Growth for me today is having the courage to say yes. Two years ago, my wife Cameron and I took our vows of membership into this church. Neither of us had ever been practicing Christians. We promised to be loyal with our prayers, our presence, our gifts, and our service. However, we didn't know we were on our way to active Christian discipleship.

During new member orientation, Chuck Gadd spoke of the opportunity of making this big church a personal and more intimate experience through involvement with Sunday school. James Loftin, minister of discipleship, told about small growth groups — eight weeks of study in Christian literature and the Bible. We signed up for a small growth group and studied Chuck Colson's *Transforming Society,* which challenged my Christian walk with a call to action.

So just a few months later I was reading the *Courier* [our Church newspaper], and saw a tiny notice where James Loftin and a few members were going to Shelby County Jail to lead a chapel service. I literally put the paper down and cringed at the thought of this. Then another voice spoke soft and firm: "That's why you need to go." So I did.

After the blessing of this first visit, I continued to go each month. Once I led the singing. (My wife reminded me I was playing for a captive audience.) On another occasion I held the chapel service myself, which became my first public witness for Christ. I have acted as the liaison for the church to Prison Fellowship Ministries this year. The Angel Tree project is under way for the children of the prisoners. We'll pass out Christmas presents and witness for Christ. Ask your Sunday school president if your class is interested in adopting a child.

I love my Sunday school class. They elected me the missions coordinator. As a class we've adopted a homeless family who is in Metropolitan InterFaith Association [an emergency housing program] and support a variety of other mission projects, each one challenging the growth of our class members.

The missions work has not been without obstacles; outside circumstances have blocked efforts. Sometimes my friends and I have disagreed. I reflected with some doubt, "Why am I doing this, for

God's glory or mine? Or, am I trying to earn God's love? I weakened and stalled.

Today I know I can't earn God's love, because Jesus already loves me. And like the song says, little ones (like me) to him belong. I am weak and he is strong. Yes, Jesus loves me. Yes, he loves me. On his strength I rely. I believe he saved me from a dark and lonely death — to use me for his good purpose. So I serve the Lord with gladness because I know it pleases him. I believe God has used this church to help discipline me to do his will. Praise God for the many colors of his loving grace. . . . .

Thanks to Jesus for his love. Thanks to this church and all of you for welcoming me into the body of Christ and encouraging me to grow in his Grace. God bless."

That makes the case doesn't it? Ron's understanding of the gospel was continually deepened by his stepping forward to trust and follow as much of Christ as he already knew. He was evangelized as he was discipled, and his growth as a disciple made him a more effective evangelist. Evangelism and discipleship go together, for there is no salvation without discipleship. Ideas have consequences: Consequences shape ideas.

Faith and Love

What do I mean by all of this in terms of the nature of evangelism as "discipleship evangelism"? First, I mean that we can't claim Jesus as Savior without a willingness to surrender to him as Lord.

Second, I mean that an emphasis on faith that does not include fidelity to Christ's call to walk in newness of life and to share that life with others is a distortion of the gospel. Faith which does not give attention to holy living and ethical issues — to telling the truth, seeking to live morally clean lives, shunning evil, fighting personal immorality and social injustice, feeding the hungry, caring for the needy, seeking the lost, suffering for those to whom the world has said no — that kind of faith, a faith that does not give attention to holy living and ethical issues, and does not care for others, is dead (James 2:26).

Third, I mean that a faith that emphasizes holy living, ethics, and good works as a saving way of life is a false faith. Does that sound contradictory to what I have just been saying? What do I mean? I mean that holy living, ethics, and good works do not save us, but rather are the evidence of the transforming work of the Spirit within us.

One of the best definitions of practical Christianity that you will find comes from the apostle Paul. It is this: *faith working through love.*

In Galatians 5:6, Paul makes the case for the essentials of the Christian life, over against the superficial claims of religious preference: "For in Christ Jesus neither circumcision nor uncircumcision counts for anything; the only thing that counts is faith working through love."

J. B. Phillips translates this "faith which expresses itself in love." The New English Bible reads "faith active in love." Paul is saying that, in God's judgment according to Christ, the question is not whether we are obedient to the law — whether we are circumcised or uncircumcised, whether we are Methodist or Baptist. The question is whether in faith we have been shaped according to the reality of God's love expressed ultimately in his crucified Son. And when there is a testing of that faith, it will involve not the doctrinal positions to which we have given intellectual ascent, not even the doctrine of the uniqueness of Christ, but whether our faith has expressed itself in love.

The goal of every church should be to have a congregation of disciples who are on a mission of discipleship. Disciples making disciples, that is the essence of evangelism. At Christ United we don't have a church-full, but we have some, and the number is growing.

Let me tell you about one of our prize examples, Pauline Hord. We celebrated Pauline's eighty-fifth birthday last April. What a celebration! Pauline is a remarkable woman. She is the most unique blending of prayer and personal piety, with servant ministry and social concern, I know. When grave needs arise in my life, Pauline is one of the first persons I call, inviting her to pray with me.

Pauline is always going to someone or some group to give herself in prayer. Hardly a week passes that I do not receive a call from Pauline, telling me about some particular need in our congregation or in our city — a need that may call for emergency housing, or transportation, or medical attention. I don't know how she is in touch with all of this, but she is.

Pauline's current passion is literacy and prison ministry. Our state, Tennessee, has a tremendous literacy problem. Thousands of people in our city can't read and write well enough to function in an adequate way in society. Pauline is working with our public schools, training teachers in a new literacy method. She gives three days a week, four or five hours a day, to teaching this new method of literacy in model programs.

But, also, once a week she drives over a hundred miles one way to Parchman State Prison down in Mississippi, to teach prisoners how to read and write. Along with this, she ministers to them in a more encompassing way as she shares her love and faith, and witnesses to the power of the gospel. Now, remember, she is eighty-five years old.

Sometime ago, President George Bush started a program in the United States called "Points of Light." He was calling for citizens to exercise positive and creative influence and service in the areas where they lived. In the different cities and communities of America, people were recognized for being "points of light." I nominated Pauline Hord for that honor, and she was written up in our daily newspaper.

A few months ago, President Bush came to Memphis. He wanted to honor the seven most outstanding "points of light" in our city — the people who had done the most for the sake of humankind. Pauline Hord was one of those selected. The President invited these seven to have lunch with him when he came for his visit to Memphis.

But, he made a mistake. He set the luncheon on a Wednesday. That's the day Pauline spends at Parchman Prison in Mississippi, teaching prisoners to read and write, and witnessing to them of the love of Christ. She would not give that up to have lunch with the President.

That says it, doesn't it?

Disciples making disciples: this is the essence of evangelism. Real evangelism, in keeping with the commandment of Christ, cannot happen except where disciples are being made. And those who are growing in discipleship become the bearers of real evangelism. All of this takes place, as we have said, primarily in the local congregation. This will be our final focus in the next lecture when we look at the church as evangelist.

■

LECTURE 3

The Church as Evangelist

■

■

LECTURE THREE

THE CHURCH AS EVANGELIST

Introductory Comments

Most of you know the name Will Campbell. He's a sort of renegade Baptist preacher who calls himself a "steeple dropout." He's a preacher without a pulpit, and he ministers to people in some of the most interesting and fascinating ways. He has been a civil rights activist, a prison reform advocate, yet a priest to members of the Ku Klux Klan. He was the minister to the University of Mississippi at the height of the civil rights movement back in the Sixties, and worked with the National Council of Churches in the civil rights movement following his time at Ole Miss. He became disillusioned with the way the National Council did ministry, feeling that they were far more sociological than they were theological, so he became a "minister at large."

Will lives on a small farm in Mt. Juliet, Tennessee, near where I lived for ten years when I was with *The Upper Room.* He lectures all over the nation, and he writes books. His best book is the first one he ever wrote entitled *Brother to a Dragonfly.* It's at once a sensitive biography and a compelling novel.[1]

In this book, Will shares a confrontation with P.D. East, an agnostic friend, the editor of a little radical newspaper in Petal, Mississippi, whom I got to know during my student days at the University of Southern Mississippi. P. D. compared the church to an Easter chicken. Let me share that with you from Will's book.

> You know, Preacher Will, that Church of yours and Mr. Jesus is like an Easter chicken my little Karen got one time. Man, it was a pretty thing. Dyed a deep purple. Bought it at the grocery store. . . . But pretty soon that baby chicken started feathering out. You know, sprouting little pin feathers. Wings and tail and all that. And you know what? Them new feathers weren't purple. No siree bob, that damn chicken wasn't really purple at all. That damn chicken was a Rhode Island Red. And when all them little red feathers started growing out from under that purple it was one hell

33

of a sight. All of a sudden Karen couldn't stand that chicken anymore. . . . Well, we took that half-purple and half-red thing out to her Grandma's house and threw it in the chicken yard with all the other chickens. It was still different, you understand. That little chicken. And the other chickens knew it was different. And they resisted it. . . . Pecked it, chased it all over the yard. Wouldn't have anything to do with it. Wouldn't even let it get on the roost with them. And that little chicken knew it was different too. It didn't bother any of the others. Wouldn't fight back or anything. Just stayed by itself. Really suffered too. But little by little, day by day, that chicken came around. Pretty soon, even before all the purple grew off it, while it was still just a little bit different, that damn thing was behaving just about like the rest of them chickens. Man, it would fight back, peck the hell out of the ones littler than it was, knock them down to catch a bug if it got to it in time. Yes siree bob, the chicken world turned that Easter chicken around. And now you can't tell one chicken from another. They're all just alike. The Easter chicken is just one more chicken. There ain't a damn thing different about it.[2]

Will knew that P.D. wanted to argue, so he didn't want to disappoint him: "Well, P.D., the Easter chicken is still useful. It lays eggs, doesn't it?" That's exactly what P.D. wanted him to say,

Yeah, Preacher Will. It lays eggs. But they all lay eggs. Who needs a Easter chicken for that? And the Rotary Club serves coffee. And the Four-H Club says prayers. The Red Cross takes up offerings for hurricane victims. Mental health does counseling, and the Boy Scouts have youth programs.[3]

I share the story to put the question about the nature of the church in perspective. Unfortunately, Will's friend is right. Too many congregations are like an Easter chicken, painted up a little bit on the outside, but the same as other chickens when the color's gone — a gathering of people who do not have that distinctive mark of Jesus upon them.

A Brief Review

In my first lecture, I opened up the relation between word and deed, dogma and experience, ideas and their consequences. We saw that what we think about Jesus Christ, his uniqueness, and the offer of grace to all through him, has everything to do with how we do evangelism. We also saw that, regardless of what we know or think we know about Jesus and about evangelism, unless his Spirit empowers us, our efforts are vain.

In the second lecture we expanded this to consider how word and deed go together in the lives of the evangelists as well as in the lives of the evangelized. Evangelism and discipleship go together. We will not be effective evangelists unless we rely upon the Spirit and unless our own lives reflect the life of Christ. Likewise, our evangelism will not be true to Jesus unless we call people to experience the whole gospel, for the whole person, for the whole world.

In this final lecture, then, I want to explore what all of this says about the role of the church, the gathered community, in bringing the word and deed of evangelism together. Let's look at two primary images of the church in the New Testament. These images define the work of the congregation as evangelist and show the church as kingdom community.

The People of God

The first image is that of the people of God. A passage that presents this image clearly is 1 Peter 2:9,10:

> But you are a chosen race, a royal priesthood, a holy nation, God's own people, in order that you may proclaim the mighty acts of him who called you out of darkness into his marvelous light. Once you were not a people, but now you are God's people; once you had not received mercy, but now you have received mercy.

The people of God, especially called to fulfill the purpose of God—that's the church. Notice that Peter applies all of the Old Testament images of "the people of God" to the New Testament church: "a chosen race, a royal priesthood, a holy nation." So this image grounds the church in the history of Israel. Having heard the promises of God, and knowing God's discipline and mercy, Israel also knew that it had received a distinct calling. This calling was to "declare the wonderful deeds of him who called us out of darkness into his marvelous light."

When this image is alive in our congregations, we know we are a part of God's history. And when we know that, what we do in evangelism, in mission, in worship, is not temporary. It is not a series of episodic programs. It is a part of God's working out God's purpose in history. The local church becomes a kingdom community.

Ben Johnson reminds us that "God's people have always carried in their hearts the dream of a kingdom, a kingdom of justice, equality, and wholeness — the purpose of God made actual in history. Evangelism inspired by the people-of-God motif can never leap irresponsibly into eternity avoiding the struggle for righteousness and justice here and now."[4]

One of the most important characteristics of "the people of God" image is *fellowship*. We belong. We belong to Christ, and we belong to each other. We are a part of a kingdom people whose roots stretch back to creation, to God's call to Abraham, and with hope stretching forward to a time when all the people of God will be gathered in the kingdom for a heavenly banquet. When this image comes alive in our local congregations, our church will begin to look more like *the church*.

John Wesley emphasized this dimension of fellowship in the way he structured the Methodist movement. He had an exceedingly strong doctrine of the church. His commitment to the church was unquestioned. He remained a priest in the Church of England. He resisted the idea of the Methodist movement becoming a church. He urged all the members of the Methodist societies to stay in communion with and to receive the sacraments of the Church of England. All this and his total life demonstrated his love and commitment to the established church.

Yet Wesley knew that it took more than hearing the Word and participating in the sacraments for Christian growth and discipleship. A deep fellowship for mutual encouragement, examination, accountability, and service was essential. Wesley talked about one loving heart setting another heart on fire. And that's a powerful image.

There is an apocryphal story of how Tallulah Bankhead went into St. Mary the Virgin Episcopal Church (I think that's in Manhattan). The church is supposed to be so "high" liturgically that Roman Catholics go there to see what it was like before all the reform of the second Vatican Council. The procession came in and it was something! It included a retired Bishop who wore a gem-studded robe and was aided by a little altar boy. The old Bishop waved a censer that emitted a cloud of incense. Tallulah, so the story goes, reached over and touched the old gentleman. Getting his attention, she said in her gravelly voice, "Dahling! Your gown is divine, but your purse is on fire."

Now that's not the kind of fire we need in the church. We need the fire of Christian fellowship, shaped and empowered by the Holy Spirit — the kind of fellowship John Wesley talked about when he talked about one loving heart setting another heart on fire. The covenant discipleship groups sponsored by the General Board of Discipleship seek to recover this kind of fellowship in one loving heart setting another heart on fire.[5]

That's a powerful image and it suggests the fact that the congregation itself becomes the witness — the evangelist. We move from seeing evangelism as a special program, or evangelistic preaching, or individual Christian witnessing, to the church itself, the fellowship, being the evangelist. In fact, the recent research of Thomas Albin suggests that our early Methodist forebears often witnessed the experience of justifying grace only after they had participated in small group experiences for a period of months or even years. What they knew *about* Christ, as a result of John Wesley's preaching, did not become real for them personally until after they had experienced the fellowship, nurture, and accountability of the people of God.[7]

What I'm calling for and what the image of the church as the people of God suggests is that the body, the community, becomes the evangelist. When the fellowship of the church comes alive by the presence of the Holy Spirit, inspiring and empowering persons to care for one another, the fellowship is redemptive within itself, and that draws people to it.

This past Christmas I received a note from a fellow in our congregation named Don Green. He's a part of our singles ministry. I heard him play the flute in our singles talent show and urged our director of music ministries to have him play in worship. He'd played in one of our Christmas services and I wrote him a note of thanks. This stimulated his note to me.

Dear Maxie:

In my adult life I've experienced events that I didn't think possible. My first wife married my best friend, my second wife killed herself, and I've been left with enormous debts. However, I discovered Christ United Methodist and Positive Christian Singles. [That's our Singles ministry.] The unconditional acceptance and true Christian love of PCS Social Singles has changed my life forever. There's no way to describe how, for the first time in my life, I'm truly happy and at peace with God and myself. I may not ever have much money, but there's no one in this church any richer!

Yours in Christ.

Don has experienced a fellowship that is redemptive within itself — not one person doing evangelism, but the fellowship, the congregation becoming the evangelist.

The Body of Christ

Now let's look at the second image of the church in the New Testament — that of the body of Christ. Paul put it graphically in Ephesians 1:20-23:

> God put this power to work in Christ when he raised him from the dead and seated him at his right hand in the heavenly places, far above all rule and authority and power and dominion, and above every name that is named, not only in this age but also in the age to come. And he has put all things under his feet and has made him the head over all things for the church, which is his body, the fullness of him who fills all in all.

Donald English tells a quaint but poignant story that speaks to this image of the church as the body of Christ.

In Birmingham, England, there is a store called Louis'. It's a great chain store in one of the main streets, and it wanted to extend. In the way of the extension was a little chapel of the Quakers, a Friends Meeting House. Louis' sent a letter to the leaders of the Friends Meeting House saying,

> Dear Sirs,
>
> We wish to extend our premises. We see that your building is right in the way. We wish therefore to buy your building and demolish it so that we might expand our store. We will pay you any price you care to name. If you will name a price we will settle the matter as quickly as possible. Yours, Sincerely.

They got a letter back by reply which said,

> Dear Sirs:
>
> We in the Friends Meeting House note the desire of Louis' to extend. We observe that our building is right in your way. We would point out, however, that we have been on our site longer than you've been on yours, and we are so determined to stay where we are that we will happily buy Louis'. If therefore you would like to name a suitable price we will settle the matter as quickly as possible. Signed, Cadbury.[7]

Here's the clincher, if it has not dawned on you. The Cadburys are the great chocolate candy making people in England. They have an enormous spread of business all over the country. The Cadburys are Quakers. They could very well have bought Louis' many times over.

The point is that it is not the size of the building that counts, but who signs the letter. One thinks of Paul's word to the church at Corinth: "You are a letter of Christ . . . written not with ink but with the Spirit of the Living God" (2 Corinthians 3:3, RSV).

The church is never in a defensive position as long as we remember who we are, and *whose* we are — the body of Christ through whom he intends to become head over everything else. Christ himself signs the letter of the church. It is Christ with whom every power in the universe must reckon, and we who make up the church are not operating out of human wisdom and strength alone. We are a new creation, a fellowship of resurrection life. We are a letter of Christ; his seal is upon us. Christ signs the letter of the church. The church is Christ's body — the fullness of him who fills all in all.

While the image of the church as the people of God suggests the dynamic of *fellowship*, the image of the church as the body of Christ speaks primarily of *serving*. Christ is present in the world through his people. Let's press that image a bit to discover how, by fulfilling this image of being the body of Christ, the congregation becomes the evangelist. What does it mean for us to be the body of Christ?

It's hard to find images that are adequate for this kind of reality, but here is one that hints at it. I was counseling with a young woman, Leigh Hobson, who had recently lost one of the most important persons in her life — an aunt who was almost a mother to her. It was painful — and she had done a lot of crying, which is cleansing and healing.

One morning, Leigh's six-year-old daughter, Katie, witnessing her mother's grief, painted a picture and gave it, with some other little tokens of love, to her mom and said, "I want you to feel better."

That night when Leigh was tucking Katie into bed, she thanked her and told her that her love gifts did make her feel better. Then she added, "But Katie, I want you to know that Mommy may cry a lot more, because I loved Ola so much."

"But, Mommy," Katie said, "I'm afraid you'll turn into a tear."

"Well," said Leigh, "If I turned into a tear, would you wipe me up?"

"No," said Katie, "I'd put you into my eye."

Wow! What perception and wisdom — what a picture of love. It's also a picture of identity, incarnation, and oneness. The church is the body of Christ. As the church in the local setting, we must be so identified with Christ that we will be his eyes, ears, voice, and arms, reaching out to express his love to a world that needs it so desperately.

I can never forget how the late Bishop Kenneth W. Copeland answered the question, What does it mean for us to be the body of Christ? To be the body of Christ is to be his presence in the world. To be Christ to the world means that we must see through the eyes of Christ. And what does it mean to see through the eyes of Christ? Through Christ's eyes, there is no East or West, no black or white, no slave or free, no male or female. All are one in Christ. Through Christ's eyes every person is of worth and the church must respond in loving concern for all persons. We must not be selective in our outreach, seeking only those who are like us. In Christ's eyes, every person is a person for whom Christ died.

Not only must we see through Christ's eyes, we must speak with the voice of Christ. We must speak with the voice of Christ to human beings in every situation and every condition. As I said in the previous lecture, it's not a matter of social gospel or personal gospel. It's a matter of the good news of Jesus Christ. War and peace, inflation and the national deficit, how the government spends the taxes we pay, where and how people live, abortion, pornography, homosexuality, adultery and fornication, ethnic relationships — whatever is of concern to human beings is a concern to the gospel. The gospel has something to say for our human plight, whether that plight involves our politics or our economics. You can't forbid the gospel from going into any area of human life. No area is off limits to Christ.

So the church must speak fearlessly and compassionately the words of God's good news to every person, wherever that person is. Not only must the church see through the eyes of Christ and speak through the voice of Christ, the church must heal with hands of Christ. The ministry of the church is the ministry of redemption and healing.

Let me illustrate with a dramatic story of redemption and healing from our congregation.

Regularly, we invite persons to witness in our worship service. Linda Malone was one of those witnesses a few months ago. She talked about the transformation she had experienced during the past year. We used words like *confused, homeless, lost,* and *dead* to describe her life before she found Jesus — no, before Jesus found her through some young couples in our church.

Tom and Claudia Twardzik had become part of our church a few years ago. He came "on profession of faith," she from Roman Catholicism. I don't know a better way to say it: they became "fired up for Jesus." They were intentional about their openness and commitment to grow, so they joined a Sunday school class and became part of one of our growth groups.

Two Christmases ago, they decided they wanted to do something for a needy family. Because of their background, they went to Catholic services. They were given the name of Linda Malone, a woman with two children who was pregnant with a third. Her husband, an addict, had deserted her. She had no place to live. A man she met in a bar offered to let her and the children move in with him "if she would keep the house clean." Social Services had told her they would come unannounced and do drug tests. If they found her using drugs, they would take the children.

The Twardziks knew this was no Christmas project, and more, they knew they couldn't do it alone. They took their concern to their Sunday school class, and to James Loftin, our minister of discipleship. The body of Christ came alive. The entire matter became a part of a local ministry, "Project Home Again," in which people commit themselves to care for one homeless family until that family is established in a place and a job. PHA deals with the homeless problem, one person or family at a time. The Twardziks kept the two children for a week while the third was being born. Other members took turns caring for the children, providing food and clothing, and persons in the group who were in recovery from alcohol or other substance abuse supported Linda as she began that agonizing struggle of recovery.

When Linda gave her witness, she had been sober for six months, had a job, and was able to be a responsible mother to her children. She was not worried about living on the streets, spending time in jail, or having her children taken away from her. Not only did she use words in her witness such as *confused, homeless, lost,* and *dead,* she used *joy, love, direction, coming home, life, saved by Jesus Christ.* It was one of the most powerful witnesses I have ever heard.

Linda has been free of drugs for about two years at the time of this writing. She is in her third job now — each one better than the previous. She has a clean, adequate apartment, and an old but dependable car that gets her back and forth to work.

Almost every Sunday, Linda and her children are on the third row on the pulpit side of our sanctuary at the 8:30 A.M. worship service. Tom and Claudia and other members of her Sunday school class are usually nearby. After 8:30 worship she teaches a three-year-old Sunday school class. She is there every Sunday and the children love her. She writes me a letter every couple of months, expressing gratitude and joy and signaling the growth taking place in her life. In one of her recent letters she said, "If you know anyone who doubts that Jesus is alive, let them talk to me."

Linda has been redeemed and healed by the hands of Christ. Do you see it?

I've said two things. As the people of God, the church is fellowship — a fellowship of the Holy Spirit, inspired and empowered to care for one another which makes the fellowship redemptive within itself. As the body of Christ, the church is Christ's incarnation in the world — a servant reaching out to be the eyes, the voice, and the hands of Jesus. When those images fulfill themselves in the life of our church, our church becomes more like *the* church. The church itself becomes the evangelist.

It may be helpful to recognize very briefly at this point the larger theological structure of all that we have said thus far. What we have really done is to articulate, from the standpoint of the local congregation, a trinitarian understanding of evangelism — centered in Jesus Christ, empowered by the Holy Spirit, and ultimately grounded in the God of all creation. The power and purpose of this God — alive and active throughout history, named in scripture and worshiped today as Father, Son, and Holy Spirit — is what finally accounts theologically for the kind of evangelism that we have been exploring. An evangelism born in the vital connection of word and deed, nurtured in the life of discipleship, and reaching toward maturity in the fellowship of the gathered community and its service in the world, is — theologically speaking — an evangelism properly tuned to the praise, power, and purpose of the triune God.

With that understanding of the church as evangelist, grounded in full trinitarian theology, I want to become very concrete again, and to talk about two audiences that clamor for the witness of the church. These are not the only two audiences that might be named, but are suggestive of how we need to discover real, flesh-and-blood, target audiences in our communities to whom we will give special attention, if we are to finally and fully live into the trinitarian structure of God's love for the world in Christ. These two audiences will demonstrate the witness of the church as fellowship and as servant — as people of God, and as the body of Christ.

The Recovering Community

The first audience is the *recovering community.* This is one of the biggest phenomena in our day — the dynamic of twelve step recovery programs. The number of people needing this help is mindboggling. There are an estimated 12 to 15 million alcoholics in the U.S. There are maybe as many millions addicted to other drugs. Millions of people are participating in twelve step recovery groups. Sometimes when I speak at conferences, and plan to touch on this issue, I will ask how many people in the audience have a family member or a close family friend who has a problem with alcohol or some other drug. Always, over 50 percent will raise their hands and often, as many as 90 percent.

When I ask the additional questions, how many of you know someone who is either in Alcoholics Anonymous or some other twelve step recovery program, over half the audience will raise hands.

I believe that this is a ministry with which the church must identify. I see more transformation taking place through twelve step programs than I see anywhere else in society today.

I never will forget a celebration we had at our church last year. We have a program in our church called "Celebrations." Two or three times a year, we bring in outstanding nationally known persons as speakers. We have brought in such people as Scott Peck, Tilden Edwards, Chuck Colson, and music groups such as Acappella. I think the most exciting time we've ever had with one of these Celebrations was when Father Joseph Martin spoke. He's probably the best known person in the United States speaking on the A.A. circuit.

Our church was packed to overflowing the night he came. There were over 2000 people there, and I've never felt that our church was more like what the church ought to be, in terms of who was present that night, as I did on that occasion. There were black folks and white folks, rich folks and poor folks, young and old, well dressed and rather shabbily dressed, liberal and conservative. It was a conglomeration of humanity, and I thought how Jesus would be pleased with this.

Our church is getting to be known in Memphis as a place of hospitality for recovering people. We have a Christian recovery group in our church. When we built our new facilities, we set aside three large rooms that would be used primarily for Alcoholics Anonymous, Narcotics Anonymous, and other groups that are reaching out to addicted folks.

In September, we had Kitty Dukakis speak; and in October, our church helped sponsor an all-day seminar on self-esteem which was focused in part on the recovering community. We sponsored this in conjunction with a local hospital that specializes in substance abuse treatment and with a weekly newspaper in our city called "Recovery Times."

The huge (and growing) community of recovering addicts needs the love and care of the church, and the explicit witness of Jesus Christ as the Incarnation of "the higher power" which can provide the resources for a life of sobriety. The image of the church that provides this is that of the people of God — a fellowship, a place of hospitality and belonging.

One of my treasured Christmas cards had this sentence penned below the formal printed greeting: "I came to this church a drunk, and you accepted me. I'm still a drunk and you accept me. But, praise God,

I'm recovering — and it is the fellowship and acceptance of the church that is empowering my change."

It's a big audience — the recovering community — and they need the church. If our church is to become more like *the* church — rooted and grounded in the love and purpose of the triune God — then we will continue and will grow in reaching out to this kind of audience.

Ministry with the Poor

The second audience that clamors for our attention is the poor. To think in terms of the poor being an audience for the church is to act as the body of Christ, God's servant in the world. When we give attention to this audience, the style must be incarnational. But before I pursue that, let me sound two warnings.

First, we must not idolize the poor to the point of making them sinless, perfect beings. The poor and the rich are both sinners in need of being reconciled to God. The poor do not automatically qualify for the kingdom of God, anymore than anyone else does. As Theodore Williams has said, "While we must do all we can to see that the poor find liberation from oppression, poverty, hunger, and sin, we must remember that we cannot bring in the utopia of perfect justice and peace. Though we believe in the present reality of the kingdom of God in our midst, we also believe in its future realization when there will be perfect justice and peace and there will be no poverty, hunger, or oppression."[8]

The second warning I would sound is this: We must resist the tendency to institutionalize our concern for the poor. We've done too much of that already. Again, Williams says,

> We build hospitals to express our concerns for the sick, orphanages to express our concerns for the orphans, homes for widows, to express our concerns for the widows, and hand over our responsibilities to these institutions, absolving ourselves of costly personal involvement. These institutions have grown independently from the church, and many have lost the original sense of mission. In many places, they've become institutions for the elite and do not cater to the poor. In the hands of a few power managers, some of them have become centers of injustice and exploitation.[9]

Too often, the involvement of the church with the poor is not unlike that of a philanthropist handing out charity. We must change that. The concern must be expressed in personal involvement, in the style of servanthood.

Now it's hard to do this, and we fail far more often than we succeed, especially in churches such as my congregation in Memphis —

an upper-middle-class congregation. I know church growth people talk about homogeneous congregations, and I know that's the way church growth often happens. But that does not excuse us from seeking to minister to the poor, in ways that avoid institutionalizing this ministry, in ways that include becoming personally involved.

Let me share two stories out of our experience at Christ Church — one completed, the other in process.

A few years ago we became convicted about the need to do evangelism among the poor black people of our city. We learned rather quickly that we could not do this ourselves in terms of the kind of identification needed for evangelism. So, we looked around, located a preacher who happened to be a Baptist, in Pine Bluff, Arkansas — a preacher who had worked with Prison Fellowship, who was street-wise, and who had a heart for the poor. We brought him to Memphis, put him on our staff, though he worked through the Methodist Neighborhood Centers. Billy Joe Jackson was his name, and he talked about economic evangelism.

He started a program which he called "Willing Workers." It was a program which picked up poor people off the street — primarily black men — men who had no jobs and couldn't make a living. He would pick them up off the street and link them up with people in our church who had short-term jobs to be done — day labor. But he did more than that. Those who became his willing workers were a part of a prayer study group that would meet weekly. Those who were willing were also linked up in a prayer partnership with some person in our church. That prayer partnership was more than prayer, it was a ministry of encouragement and support. It required that the partner from our church be available and try to help in every way possible this person who was looking for a way to make a living and to get his or her life in order.

One of the first persons who became a part of the Willing Worker program was a man named Charles Hall. Charles was not long out of jail, and he had no family. He was living from hand to mouth, sleeping wherever he could. I don't even know how Billy Joe located him. But he became a willing worker. He was assigned a prayer partner in our church, a fellow named Fred Mills. Fred met with Charles once a week, tutored him in a lot of different skills, discovered him to be a very responsible person, and suggested to us that he was the kind of person who, should there be an opening on the staff of our church in the maintenance department, would be a good candidate. Sure enough, that happened and Charles came to work for us.

But something had happened in the meantime in the prayer study group. Charles had been converted. He accepted Christ as his personal Savior. And one of the great joys of my life was to share in his baptism.

But that is not all. Charles became a Christian, and he came to work for us at the church. Along the way, he got married. He married a woman who had three children. During that time, our church had also started working with Habitat for Humanity. We had participated with other churches and groups in building houses for the working poor. Then we took it on ourselves to raise the money and build a house all by ourselves. We have built three Habitat houses and are committed to building one each year. Would you believe that the person who bought that house was Charles Hall? It's one of the most complete stories that I've ever been a part of. Charles was picked up off the street and became a responsible citizen, earning his own living. He became a Christian, and is now a homeowner. He is still working in our church — has been on our staff now for about seven years and is a very productive person.

The stories don't always turn out that way and nobody knows that better than I do. We fail far more than we succeed. But, we're not promised success in our ministry; we are called to be faithful and that calling is pretty clear according to Jesus. "Inasmuch as you did it unto the least of these — the poor, the homeless, the prisoner — inasmuch as you've done it unto the least of these you've done it unto me."

The second story is just beginning, but I'm excited about it. When we built our new facilities two years ago, we planned for a childcare ministry. We were doing a Parents' Day Out program twice a week, but felt that child care was one of the critical needs of our city and one of the critical needs of the nation. So we built our facilities in a way that we could expand our program and have a full week-long approved childcare program — as well as expand our Parents' Day Out. In doing so, we knew that we would primarily be ministering in our community which, as I said earlier, is a middle to upper-middle class community. But we felt we could not, in all good conscience, seeking to be faithful to the gospel, put so much energy and resources in that ministry without ministering in a similar way in a needy area of our city. So we decided that we would make a commitment to minister to children in the inner city. If there was profit made from the daycare or Parents' Day Out program, we would use that to do a similar ministry in the inner city.

In the midst of thinking about that, God has given us a vision of a private school that will primarily serve at-risk children in the inner city — those children who are dropping through the cracks of the public school system. We were inspired by the Marva Collins model in Chicago and other innovative education efforts focused on the poor and the at-risk. But we wanted ours to be explicitly Christian, and we've designed it that way. The groundwork has been laid for the "Shepherd School," and we're going to start next September. It will be a school with an integrated curriculum and a kind of one-room schoolhouse approach where at-risk children will get the opportunity to have the attention that children in the private schools of our nation get. We will start out with forty-five children, and if it's successful, which we're certain it's going to be, our idea is that we'll have a number of these little centers set down in different areas of our city where children are at risk, and where they need somebody to pay special attention to them.

As an explicitly Christian school, motivated by the servant mind of Christ, I can't imagine anything that is more clearly an expression of evangelism.

Now you can play this out to make it relevant to your own situation. The images of the church as "the people of God" and "the body of Christ" are universally relevant. The models of ministry that grow out of those images — fellowship and service — also have universal application. What is unique in each situation is the audience that must be deliberately chosen, considered, served, and welcomed into the fellowship. Listen to another word from John McFarland, whom I quoted previously.

> The only way to do evangelism is just to do it. Sooner or later someone who is "in" must ask someone who is "out" to come to the church. Instead, most churches put new signs on their building and place ads in the paper. They create special parking spaces for "visitors." They take pies to "first-time attenders." They do everything except ask people to join. No number of denominational videos or crusades with catchy titles will cause that to happen. If we spent on inviting people into our gatherings even half the time spent on thinking up evangelism programs and having meetings to explain them, the mainline decline would end tomorrow.[10]

The Place of Personal Witness

So, let me close with a word about personal witness. With all my emphasis on the church as a whole, being the evangelist, I'm not diminishing the place of personal witness. That's one of the weaknesses of the modern church. We don't train our people to be witnesses. We've strayed from the powerful dynamic of the New Testament church in which the responsibility of being witnesses belonged to every single member. According to Michael Green,

> You find it everywhere in the New Testament. In 1 Thessalonians 1:8, Paul rejoices that the word of God has sounded forth from those newly fledged Thessalonian Christians, and their faith in God has spread like wildfire. And in Acts 8:1,4, we find the Jerusalem leaders shut up in fear in an upper room while the common believers were scattered by a persecution springing from the death of Stephen. What did they do? They went everywhere spreading the good news. It was every member ministry in those days. Evangelism was the spontaneous chattering of good news. It was engaged in naturally, continuously, easily, and joyfully by Christians wherever they went. Harnack justly remarks that the mission of the early church was in fact accomplished to a very large extent by informal missionaries. Christians would wander from hamlet to hamlet, village to village, in order to win fresh converts to their Lord.[11]

Contemporary church growth research shows that approximately 77 percent of the persons who become Christian disciples do so because of the testimony, deeds, and encouragement of someone they trust. George Morris and Eddie Fox, in their book, *Faith-Sharing,* remind us that there are three crucial issues revealed in this statistic.

> Effective faith-sharing involves a proper balance of word, deed, and encouragement. Word here is understood as proclamation and/or testimony. Deed is understood as faithful Christian lifestyle and service. Encouragement is understood as active initiative on the part of the faith-sharer. The Christian must take the initiative and do as Jesus commanded —"Go." Christians must go to the people, love the people, share word and life with the people, listen to the people, and offer Christ to the people.[12]

This suggests a crucial issue for the local church. If 77 percent of the persons who become Christian disciples do so because of the testimony, deeds, and encouragement of someone they trust, then person-to-person faith-sharing must be the highest priority, and we must train our people in this ministry. Christians must be equipped not only with the personal knowledge of Jesus Christ and a knowledge of the gospel, they must also know how to relate to another person in such a way that trust develops.

As a reminder of this, I keep an old worship bulletin from our church — our worship service on December 30, 1984. The first act of praise in our worship service that day was a solo entitled "Sing Your Praises to the Lord." This selection was composed by Don Halpern, and Don sang it that day. The chorus song goes:

> When you're lost and alone and have no place you can go,
> Nothing has worked out as planned.
> There's one who is greater, there's one who is waiting,
> Just let Jesus take your hand.
> Sing Alleluia, Alleluia
> Sing your praises to the Lord.[13]

Now that may not sound like great poetry, and the music to which it was set might not be considered great music. But I wish you had been in our service that day. Don Halpern is a bearded young man, who plays a classical guitar beautifully. I met Don about a year preceding his singing in our worship. He was Jewish. He made an appointment to see me one day, and I was amazed that he wanted to talk about Christianity at the church. He came back two or three times. Then one Sunday morning, we were celebrating Holy Communion, and I saw Don Halpern approaching the altar to receive the elements of bread and wine. The next Sunday he walked down the aisle and made a public profession of faith in Jesus Christ. I didn't baptize him that Sunday, because I wanted to talk to him. It is a big step for a Jew to make a profession of faith in Christ. I talked to him during the week and the following Sunday, not only did we baptize him, we baptized his two children.

During the Christmas season, after his profession of faith, Don sang and played "Gentle Mary laid her child lowly in a manger." What a witness! On the following Sunday, he was singing, "There's one who is greater, there's one who is waiting, just let Jesus take your hand" — singing about the Messiah.

You know what I thought of when he sang for us in that worship service. I thought about how he came to be in our church. It wasn't this preacher who really won him to Christ. It was Martha and Don Helm, a young lay couple who had had a transforming experience in our church. They were Don Halpern's neighbors. Their lives were so transformed by Christ that they captured his attention; their performance and their profession spoke to this young Jewish person, and their witness is really what won him.

Martha and Don Helm embodied the kind of evangelism we have been talking about in these three lectures — an evangelism of word and deed, centered in Christ, waiting on the power and timing of the Holy Spirit, growing in the grace of full discipleship, sharing in the to the love of God for the whole world in Christ, and empowered by the Spirit, our church is becoming more like *the church,* and we are daily witnessing the transforming power of the gospel in our world.

I've had a good time with you in this Conference. It's been great. I've learned and I've been blessed. But I hope not a single one of you will go to another evangelism conference unless and until evangelism is taking place where you live, in your local congregation. Go home and "just do it"!

ENDNOTES

LECTURE ONE: IDEAS HAVE CONSEQUENCES

1. As quoted in Ben Johnson, *An Evangelism Primer: Practical Principles for Congregations* (Atlanta, GA: John Knox Press, 1983), p. 7.

2. Donald McGavran, "Will Upsala Betray the Two Billion?" *Church Growth Bulletin,* 4 (5); reprinted in *The Conciliar-Evangelical Debate: The Crucial Documents, 1964-1976,* ed. by Donald McGavran (South Pasadena, CA: William Carey, 1977), pp. 233-241; as quoted in Norman E. Thomas, "Ecumenical Directions in Evangelism: Melbourne to San Antonio," *Journal of the Academy for Evangelism in Theological Education,* Volume Five (1989-1990), p. 52.

3. Phillip Potter, "Evangelism and the World Council of Churches," *Ecumenical Review,* 20:2 (1968), p. 171; as quoted in Norman Thomas, "Ecumenical Directions," p. 52.

4. Norman E. Thomas, "Ecumenical Directions," p. 53.

5. Ibid., p. 54.

6. Carl E. Braaten, "The Meaning of Evangelism in the Context of God's Universal Grace," *Journal of the Academy for Evangelism in Theological Education,* Volume Three (1987-1988), p. 11.

7. William R. Cannon, *The Theology of John Wesley* (New York: Abingdon Press, 1946), p. 93.

8. Braaten, "The Meaning of Evangelism," p. 15.

9. Ibid.

10. David Lowes Watson, *God Does Not Foreclose: The Universal Promise of Salvation* (Nashville: Abingdon Press, 1990), p. 94.

11. Ibid., p. 95.

12. Ibid., p. 94; quoting Braaten, "The Meaning of Evangelism," p. 17.

13. Braaten, "The Meaning of Evangelism," p. 17.

14. From the author's personal correspondence; also printed in Maxie Dunnam, *Living the Psalms: A Confidence for All Seasons* (Nashville: The Upper Room, 1990), pp. 80-81.

15. From the author's personal correspondence quoting *The Book of Common Prayer* (1979 Edition), p. 451.

16. Michael Green, *New Testament Evangelism: Lessons for Today* (Manilla: OMF Publishers, 1982; first published by Discipleship Resources, 1979), pp. 136-37.

17. Albert C. Outler, *Evangelism in the Wesleyan Spirit* (Nashville: Discipleship Resources, 1971), p. 49.

LECTURE TWO: DISCIPLESHIP EVANGELISM

1. John Robert McFarland, "What's Wrong with the 'What's Wrong' Books?", *The Christian Century* (October 23, 1991), p. 957. Copyright © 1991 Christian Century Foundation. Reprinted by permission.

2. Ibid.

3. Ibid.

4. Ibid.

5. Ibid.

6. Mortimer Arias, "The Great Commission: Mission as Discipleship," *Journal of the Academy for Evangelism in Theological Education*, Volume 4 (1988-89), p. 17.

7. Lesslie Newbegin, *Mission in Christ's Way: Bible Studies* (Geneva: WCC, 1987), p. 32; quoted in Arias, "The Great Commission," p. 17.

8. Quoted in Arias, "The Great Commission," p. 21.

9. George E. Sweazey, *The Church as Evangelist* (San Francisco: Harper and Rowe, 1978), p. 21.

10. Ibid.

11. From the Preface to *Hymns and Sacred Poems* by John and Charles Wesley; reprinted in *The Works of John Wesley,* ed. Thomas Jackson, Vol. XIV (Peabody, Mass.: Hendrickson Publishers Inc., 1984), p. 321.

12. See for example Elie Halevy, *A History of the English People in the 19th Century,* Vol. I, *England in 1815* (London: T.F. Unwin, 1924; 2nd ed., New York: Peter Smith, 1949), pp. 389-459, 588-91.

LECTURE THREE: THE CHURCH AS EVANGELIST

1. Will D. Campbell, *Brother to a Dragonfly* (New York: Continuum Publishing Company, 1985). Copyright © 1977 by Will D. Campbell. Reprinted by permission of The Continuum Publishing Company.

2. Ibid., pp. 219-20.

3. Ibid., p. 220.

4. Ben Johnson, *An Evangelism Primer: Practical Principles for Congregations* (Atlanta, GA: John Knox Press, 1983), pp. 24-25.

5. The basic handbook for covenant discipleship group members is *Covenant Discipleship: Christian Formation through Mutual Accountability* by David Lowes Watson (Nashville: Discipleship Resources, 1991, order no. DR091B). Information on the Covenant Discipleship program is available from the Section on Covenant Discipleship of the General Board of Discipleship.

6. Tom Albin, "An Empirical Study of Early Methodist Spirituality," in *Wesleyan Theology Today,* ed. Theodore Runyon (Nashville: Kingswood, 1985), pp. 275-90.

7. Donald English of the Home Mission Board of London, England, told this story when he preached at Christ United Methodist Church in Memphis, Tennessee in August 1984.

8. Theodore Williams, "Christian Solidarity with the Suffering and the Poor of the World," an address delivered at The World Methodist Conference meeting in Singapore, 1991.

9. Ibid.

10. John Robert McFarland, "What's Wrong," p. 958.

11. As quoted in Michael Green, *New Testament Evangelism,* p. 114.

12. H. Eddie Fox and George E. Morris, *Faith-Sharing: Dynamic Christian Witnessing by Invitation* (Nashville: Discipleship Resources, 1986), p. 80.

13. Unpublished song. Used by permission of Don Halpern. Copyright © 1984, "Sing your Praises to the Lord" by Don Halpern.

FOR FURTHER READING

Joseph C. Aldrich. *Life-Style Evangelism.* Portland, OR: Multnomah Press, 1981.

Mortimer Arias. *Announcing the Reign of God.* Philadephia, PA: Fortress Press, 1984.

C. John Miller. *Outgrowing the Ingrown Church.* Grand Rapids, MI: Zondervan Publishing House, 1986.

Herb Miller. *Fishing on the Asphalt: Effective Evangelism in Mainline Denominations.* St. Louis, MO: Bethany Press, 1983.

Albert C. Outler. *Evangelism in the Wesleyan Spirit.* Nashville, TN: Discipleship Resources, 1971.

Christopher C. Walker. *Connecting with the Spirit of Christ.* Nashville, TN: Discipleship Resources, 1988.

Richard M. Weaver. *Ideas Have Consequences.* Chicago and London: University of Chicago Press, 1948.